Copyright Page
Copyright © 2024 by A. Brown
All rights reserved.

No part of this book may be reproduced or transmitted in any form or by any means, electronic or mechanical, including photocopying, recording, or any information storage and retrieval system, without permission in writing from the publisher.

This book is a work of fiction. Any resemblance to actual persons, living or dead, or actual events is purely coincidental.

For information, please contact:
A. Brown
Email: abrownbooks642@gmail.com
ISBN: To Be Assigned
Published by A. Brown
Illustrations by A. Brown
First Edition

In a land where dragons soar and glide,

Lived a little dragon, named Clyde.

His scales were blue, his wings spread wide,

But there was a secret he tried to hide.

When Clyde would try to breathe out fire,

All he'd feel was fear and dire.

He worried his flames might cause despair,

So he kept them hidden with utmost care.

Clyde's friends were brave, they roamed and played,

Breathing fire in a colorful parade.

Clyde watched in awe, yet stayed behind,

Afraid of the power he might find.

One sunny day, his friend Pip the mouse,

Said, "Clyde, come out from your hiding house!

Your fire's a gift, not something to fear,

We're all here to help, to keep you near."

Clyde shook his head, with a tiny sigh,

"But what if my flames reach the sky?"

Pip patted his claw, with a smile so bright,

"Trust yourself, and you'll be alright."

Flora the fox then joined the pair,

With flowers woven in her hair.

"Your fire is part of who you are,

A little flame, like a guiding star."

Then came Benny, a bear so big,

With a gentle laugh and a playful jig.

"Clyde, your heart shines with a light so warm,

Your fire could never cause a storm."

The friends all gathered in a circle wide,

Encouraging Clyde to let go of his pride.

He took a deep breath, feeling their love,

And looked to the bright sky above.

With a gentle puff, he gave it a try,

A flicker of flame danced in the sky.

Not a roaring fire, but a little spark,

It lit up the woods, not leaving a mark.

Clyde laughed with joy, his fears set free,

His friends cheered loudly, as happy as can be.

The flames were warm, like a hug from the sun,

Clyde's heart was light, his journey begun.

The shy young dragon felt so proud,

He stood tall and strong amid his crowd.

His heart grew big with every cheer,

As he let his little flame appear.

Clyde learned that day, with friends so true,

Love and courage helped him through.

His fire was special, his heart was bright,

A little flame that felt just right.

Oh, how they danced in the evening glow,

Clyde and his friends, with hearts aglow.

The night was filled with laughter and
light,

As they celebrated into the night.

Clyde now knew what he was meant to be,

A dragon with heart, wild and free.

His flame was his own, unique and grand,

A little fire, like a warm, gentle hand.

So if you feel different, don't hide away,

Remember Clyde, and embrace your day.

Your heart is big, your light is true,

A little fire can be magic too.

The End